Life in
JAMESTOWN COLONY

By Janey Levy

Gareth Stevens
Publishing

Please visit our website, www.garethstevens.com. For a free color catalog of all our high-quality books, call toll free 1-800-542-2595 or fax 1-877-542-2596.

Library of Congress Cataloging-in-Publication Data

Levy, Janey.
Life in Jamestown Colony / by Janey Levy.
 p. cm. — (What you didn't know about history)
Includes index.
ISBN 978-1-4824-0587-3 (pbk.)
ISBN 978-1-4824-0589-7 (6-pack)
ISBN 978-1-4824-0586-6 (library binding)
1. Jamestown (Va.) — History — 17th century — Juvenile literature. 2. Virginia — History — Colonial period, ca. 1600-1775 — Juvenile literature. I. Levy, Janey. II. Title.
F234.J3 L48 2014
975.5'02—dc23

First Edition

Published in 2014 by
Gareth Stevens Publishing
111 East 14th Street, Suite 349
New York, NY 10003

Copyright © 2014 Gareth Stevens Publishing

Designer: Andrea Davison-Bartolotta
Editor: Kristen Rajczak

Photo credits: Cover, pp. 1, 19 Hulton Archive/Getty Images; p. 5 Adrin Snider/Newport Daily Press/MCT via Getty Images; p. 6 Florilegius/SSPL/Getty Images; pp. 7, 11, 16, 17 MPI/Getty Images; p. 9 (inset) Ira Block/National Geographic/Getty Images; p. 9 (main) Tim Graham/Getty Images; p. 12 Walter Bibikow/Taxi/Getty Images; pp. 13, 15 (main) Marilyn Angel Wynn/Nativestock/Getty Images; p. 15 (inset) Kean Collection/Getty Images; p. 18 Mannie Garcia/AFP/Getty Images; p. 20 Joseph Sohm- Visions of America/Stockbyte/ Getty Images.

Printed in the United States of America

CPSIA compliance information: Batch #CW14GS: For further information contact Gareth Stevens, New York, New York at 1-800-542-2595.

CONTENTS

Words in the glossary appear in **bold** type the first time they are used in the text.

1607

The year 1607 was a turning point in American history. Settlers arriving in Virginia founded the first **permanent** English colony in North America. They chose a spot about 60 miles (96.5 km) from Chesapeake Bay, on the banks of a river. They named both the James River and Jamestown Colony in honor of their king, James I.

Jamestown was the capital of Virginia, and although the early years were hard, it soon became wealthy. It sounds like a success story! But is that Jamestown's true story?

Did You Know?

The journey from England to North America took more than 4 months. The settlers spent another 2 weeks in their ships searching the coast for a good spot to land.

The ships that brought the settlers to Jamestown were named the Susan Constant, Godspeed, *and* Discovery. *Modern copies of the ships can be seen at Jamestown today.*

A GET-RICH-QUICK PLAN

The Virginia Company in London, England, provided the money to found Jamestown. In return, the company's **investors** expected riches. Settlers were to immediately start sending back lumber, glass, tar, and **sassafras**. Above all, investors wanted gold and silver.

What made investors think people would make the long journey to the colony? Many people in England couldn't find work. There were too many people and not enough jobs. Investors thought people would be happy for the chance to go to North America.

sassafras leaves

Did You Know?

Sassafras is used to make root beer and a kind of tea. In the 1600s, people in Europe believed it could cure almost any sickness and even stop people from getting old!

This painting shows what one artist thought Jamestown Colony might have looked like.

7

The first group of 104 settlers included only men and boys—there were no women! Investors probably thought this was a good idea. The first settlers needed to build homes quickly and start sending goods back to London. This would have been men's work.

The first two women arrived in October 1608. One was the wife of a settler. The other woman was her maid. More women slowly arrived. But all through the 1600s, there were more men than women in Jamestown.

Did You Know?

About one-third of the first group of settlers were "gentlemen" who lacked practical work experience. There were also carpenters, bricklayers, and a barber.

Today, people dress up as the Jamestown settlers at the living-history museum of the colony. At bottom right, a blacksmith at historic Jamestown makes an ax.

9

WHO NEEDS TO GROW FOOD?

The settlers brought tools to build houses and strong walls to keep them safe. They also had weapons to use in case of Native American attacks.

However, the settlers brought few tools for farming. They believed the same Native Americans who might attack them would be happy to supply them with food through trade. This didn't always work out. The settlers were soon hungry and sick. When the first supply ship arrived in January 1608, only 38 settlers remained.

Did You Know?
Archaeologists have found animal bones that tell them what the first settlers ate. Their food included fish, turtles, birds, and raccoons.

Some of the time, colonists in Jamestown were able to trade with local Native Americans.

11

The settlers didn't realize it, but they arrived at a bad time. A **drought** had started the year before. It was the driest time in almost 800 years, and it lasted until 1612.

Finding food in the forest was hard. The Powhatan Indians sometimes sent food to the settlers, but they didn't have much extra to share. After a while, the Powhatans became angry because the settlers demanded so much food from them. The settlers even stole food from the Powhatans!

Did-You-Know?

The spot where the settlers built Jamestown was one the Powhatans didn't want. It was **marshy** and didn't have good water for drinking.

The Powhatans ate foods such as corn, squash, nuts, beans, and berries.

THE POWHATANS

When the settlers arrived in 1607, there were 32 tribes of Powhatans in the area. They had been living in Virginia for thousands of years. The tribes lived in separate villages but had common beliefs and ways of living.

Each village had its own chief, and one head chief ruled over them all. The head chief's name was Wahunsonacock (wah-huhn-SEHN-uh-kawh). He came from the village of Powhatan, and the settlers used that name both for him and for the local Native Americans.

Did You Know?

"Powhatan" meant "waterfall" in the language of the local Native Americans. Wahunsonacock's home village was near a waterfall.

Powhatan houses were called *yehakins*. The Powhatans built a frame by bending small trees, then covered the frame with bark or mats made from marsh plants.

Native American village in Virginia

By the fall of 1609, settlers in Jamestown were **starving**. The continuing drought meant the Powhatans had less food and were no longer sending any to the settlers. In fact, the Powhatans were so angry at the settlers that they killed anyone who left Jamestown to search for food.

The settlers had to eat whatever they could find in the colony. They ate horses, dogs, rats, and poisonous snakes. They ate their boots. They even dug up dead people and ate them!

Did You Know?

60 survived

The colonists and Powhatans had an uneasy relationship from the start. While there were times of peace, the two groups also fought often.

17

Three events in 1619 shaped Jamestown and the country. The first marked the beginning of the type of government we have today. It was the earliest meeting of a **representative** government in the colonies. The second marked the beginning of slavery in the colonies. It was the arrival of the earliest recorded Africans.

The third event was the arrival of about 90 unmarried women. The Virginia Company realized families were necessary to make Jamestown permanent, so they sent women to marry the colony's men and raise children.

a woman in colonial dress

This image shows the arrival of the first Africans to Jamestown.

Did You Know?

The first Africans were likely treated as **indentured servants** rather than slaves. However, by around the mid-1600s, it had become usual for Africans to be slaves for life.

THE END OF JAMESTOWN

As Jamestown grew, settlers occupied more and more Powhatan land. Angry Powhatans began a war in 1622. In 1624, King James I made Virginia a royal colony. Jamestown remained the capital, and tobacco farms helped it grow larger.

In 1698, fire burned down the statehouse in Jamestown. Williamsburg then became the capital. People continued to live at Jamestown, but it was no longer a town. By the 1750s, Jamestown had disappeared, and the land was used for farming.

present-day
Jamestown, Virginia

A Timeline of Jamestown

10,000 BC	**Ancestors** of Powhatans arrive in Virginia
1600	About 25,000 Powhatans live in Virginia
1606	Drought starts
1607	Virginia Company founds Jamestown as capital of Virginia
1608	First two women arrive
1609–1610	Starving Time
1622	Powhatans start war
1624	King James I makes Virginia a royal colony
1698	Statehouse burns down
1699	Jamestown no longer the capital
1750s	Jamestown no longer exists

LOSSARY

ancestor: someone in a family who lived long ago

archaeologist: someone who studies objects and buildings to learn about life in the past

drought: a long period of time with little rain

indentured servant: someone who works for another person for a set time in exchange for travel expenses

investor: someone who spends money on something and expects to get more money back

marshy: having soft, wet land

permanent: lasting a long time

representative: having to do with a system in which citizens vote for people to serve in government and make decisions for them

sassafras: a tree common to eastern North America whose leaves and bark were used to treat sickness and flavor food and drink

starve: to suffer or die from lack of food

FOR MORE INFORMATION

Books

Harkins, William H., and Susan Sales Harkins. *Jamestown: The First English Colony.* Hockessin, DE: Mitchell Lane Publishers, 2007.

Higgins, Melissa. *The Jamestown Colony.* Minneapolis, MN: ABDO Publishing, 2013.

Lange, Karen E. *1607: A New Look at Jamestown.* Washington, DC: National Geographic, 2007.

Websites

On the Trail of Captain John Smith
kids.nationalgeographic.com/kids/games/interactiveadventures/john-smith/
Learn about Jamestown and John Smith in this interactive adventure!

Powhatan Indian Fact Sheet
www.bigorrin.org/powhatan_kids.htm
Find out more about the Powhatan Indians and their way of life on this website about Native Americans.